Vroom!

HOT SUVS

GMC YUKON DENALI

TABLE OF CONTENTS

The Yukon Denali weighs 5,965 pounds (2,706 kilograms), yet can go from zero to 60 miles (96.56 kilometers) per hour in only 5.8 seconds.

JUST GREAT

The GMC Yukon Denali is named after Canada's Yukon River and Alaska's Denali Mountain. Yukon means "Great River" and Denali means "Great Mountain." It's easy to imagine the big SUV tearing across an icy stream or climbing up a snow-covered mountain. It's also easy to imagine the Yukon Denali roaring down a dusty desert road or cruising along a city street.

ENGINE POWER

The Yukon Denali looks powerful for good reason. Beneath its hood, like a sleeping tiger, purrs a big **V-8** engine. It produces 365 **horsepower** and 383 pound-feet (519 Newton-meters) of **torque**. That gives the Denali about four times the horsepower and four times the torque of an average car. This muscle allows the Denali to tow up to 8,500 pounds (3,855.5 kilograms).

That's as heavy as an adult African elephant or two full-size cars.

BEAUTY ON THE INSIDE

The GMC Yukon Denali may be a beast on the highway. But inside it's more like a **stylish** and luxurious hotel room that sits nine passengers.

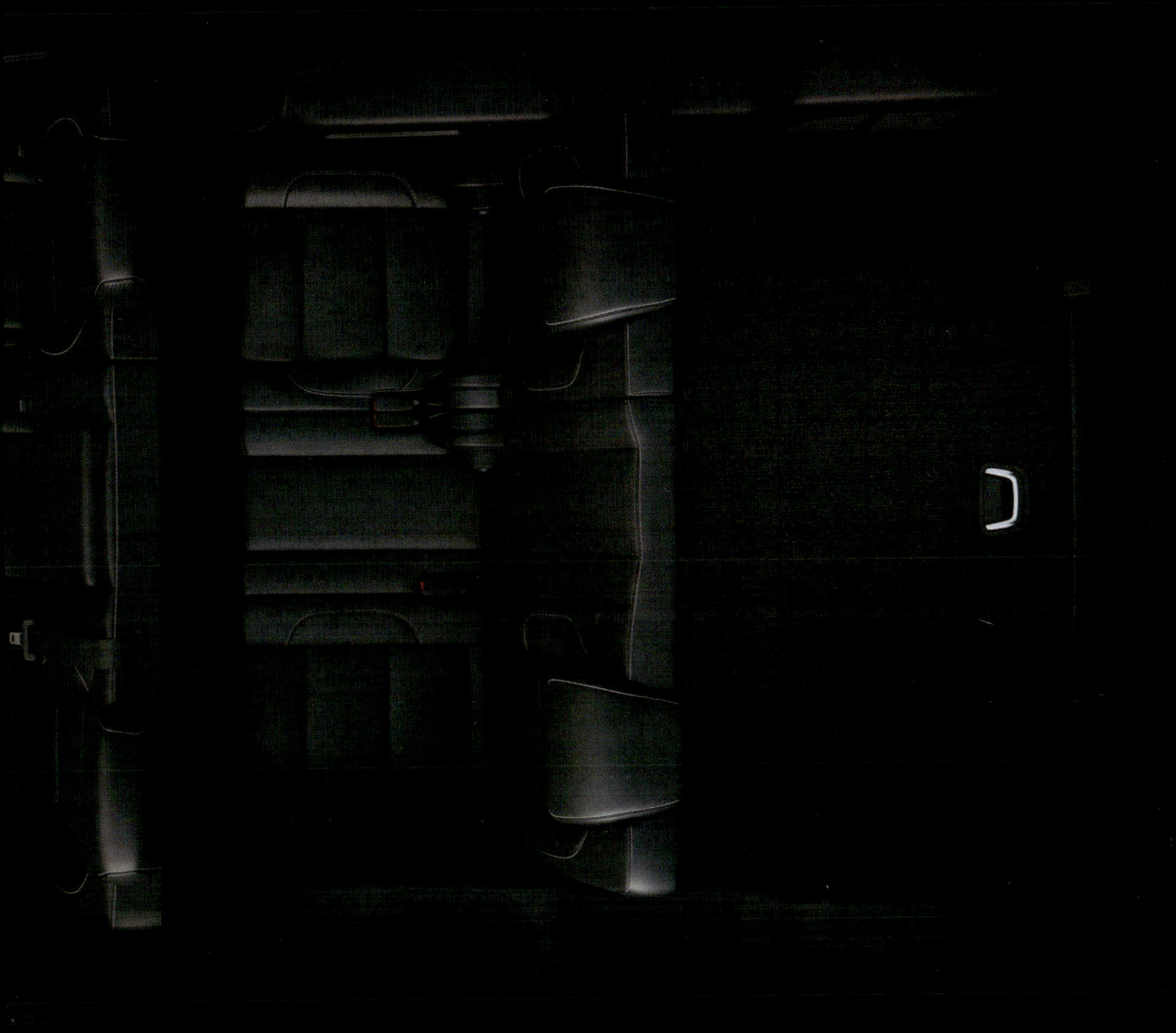

Soft lights illuminate all its door handles. Its seats are heated for cold days and cooled for hot days.

Much of the interior of the Yukon Denali features leather. The driver's seat and front passenger seat also have power adjusters to produce 12 levels of seating comfort.

Press a button and the Denali's heated steering column will rise up to where you want it and tilt to where it is most comfortable. The Denali also has **tri-zone** climate control. That means that just about everyone in the cabin can have his or her own heating and air conditioning.

Ready, set, launch! The steering wheel and dashboard of the Denali just ask for action.

DENALI

SMOOTH AND SILENT

Despite its large size, the Denali's ride is both smooth and quiet. The secret is its Magnetic Ride Control (MRC) shock absorbers. The Denali has magnetized fluids with sensors on each of its four wheels to pick up even the smallest changes in the surface of the road. Information instantly goes to an electronic control unit (ECU). This allows the ECU to adjust the Denali's ride to smooth out any bump in the road.

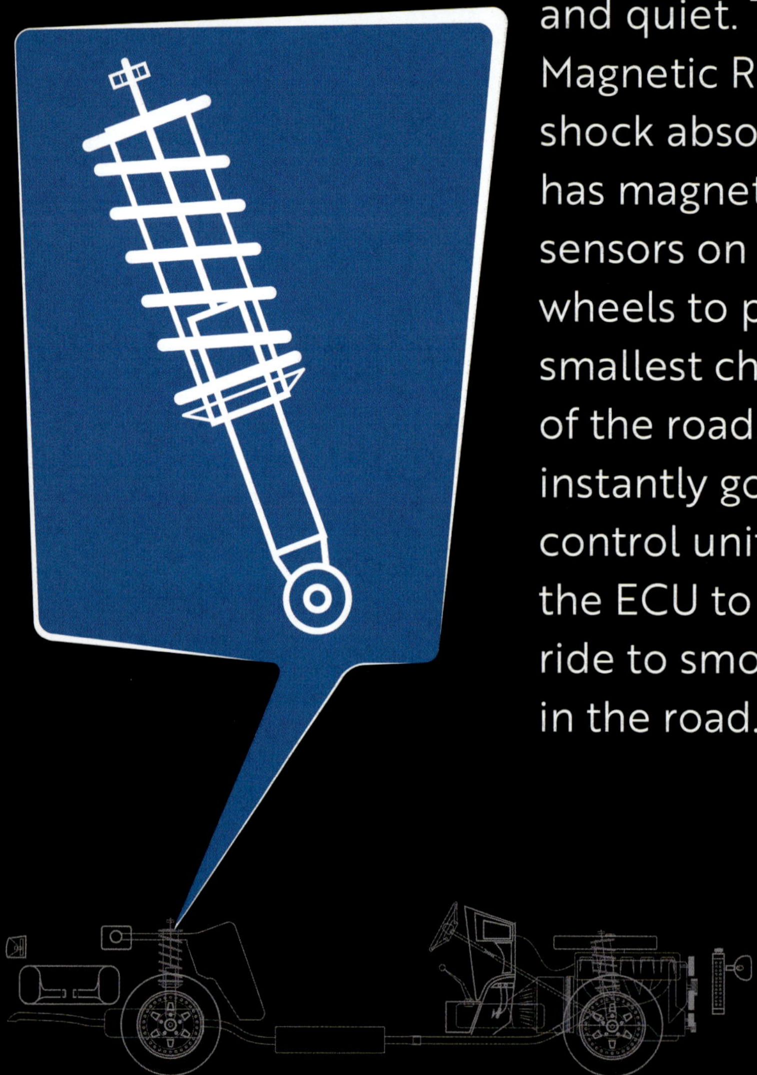

Shock absorbers are devices designed to eliminate the bumps caused by rough roads. Cars have a shock absorber on each wheel.

The Denali automatically adjusts its shock absorbers ten times faster than the blink of an eye!

Other features include keyless ignition, a hands-free power liftgate, illuminated outside door handles, and heated outside mirrors. It also has a roomy 26 square feet (2.4 square meters) of **cargo** space with its rear seats folded down.

It's easy. Just touch a button to open and close the Denali's lift gate.

Wide open spaces—the Denali has plenty of room to carry a wide variety of objects.

The Denali also offers a Bose Centerpoint surround sound system that makes driving feel like sitting in the middle of a live concert.

GM was the first automobile company to enclose passengers and driver. At the time, most cars were like "horseless carriages" with everyone sitting in the open.

DRIVE AND SHOP

An added feature in newer Denali models allows drivers to shop on the go. "Marketplace" is an app that appears on GM's dashboard screen. Pressing the icon allows drivers to order coffee, make restaurant reservations, or even buy burgers and chicken wings. GM says Marketplace is designed to be safer than using the phone while driving.

Let's order breakfast! Just press the icon and it will be ready at your favorite restaurant.

Staying Connected

The Denali's dashboard screen also serves as a multi-color driver information center. Driver and passengers can stay in touch even if they're in the middle of nowhere. The screen connects the entire cabin to the Internet and to all important parts of the SUV inside and out. Wi-Fi is on whenever the car is turned on and it supports up to seven mobile phones and computers.

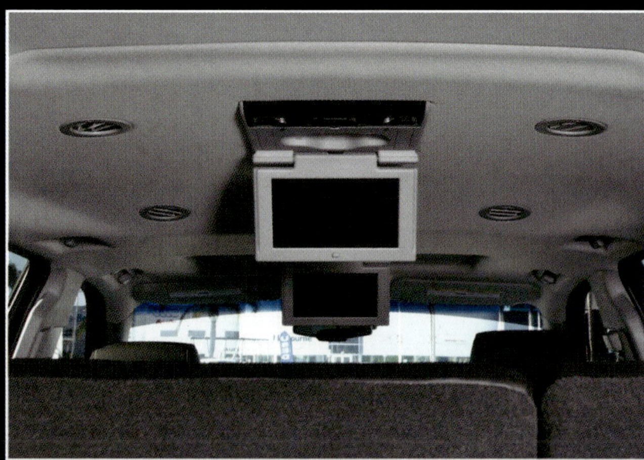

The Denali can come with three touch screens—one for each row of seats.

It's hard to get lost in a Denali. Just touch the screen to see where you are on the road.

SENSORS AT WORK

The Denali is seven feet (2.13 meters) wide and 18.7 feet (5.7 meters) long. To help drivers park this large vehicle, GMC added special features. **Proximity** sensors tell the Denali driver how close he or she is to a parked car in front and in back.

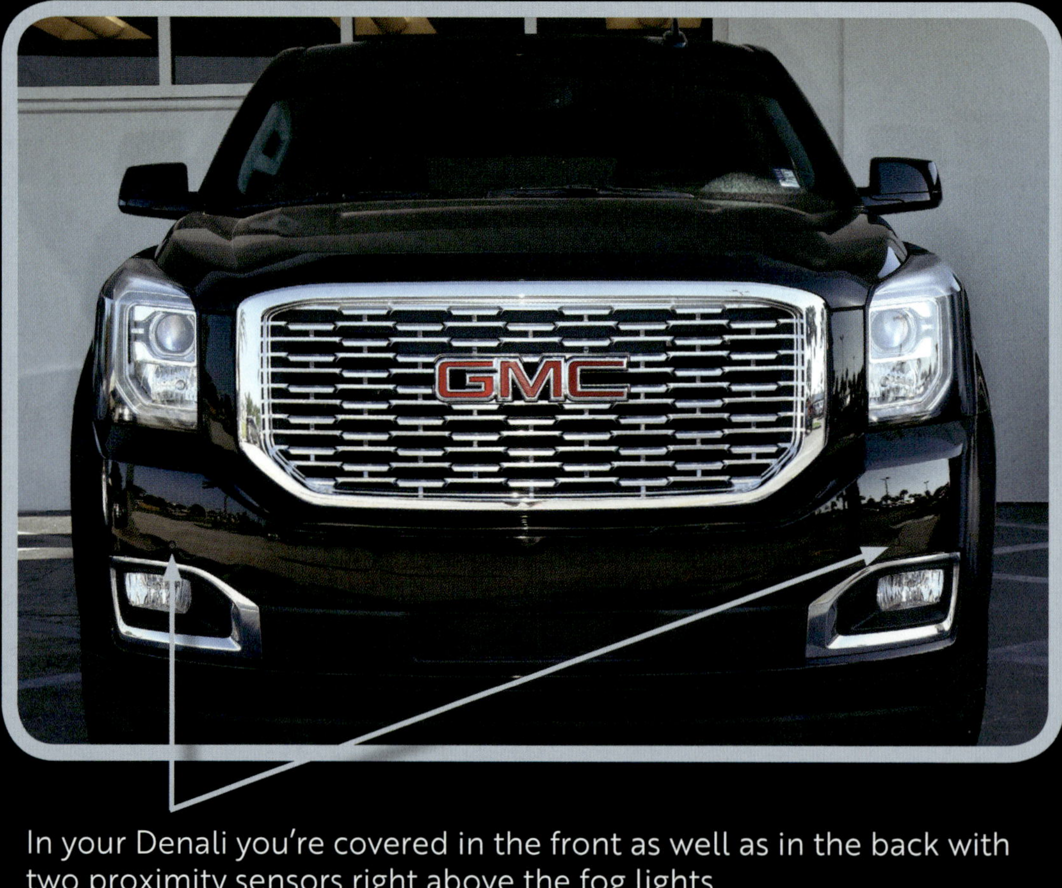

In your Denali you're covered in the front as well as in the back with two proximity sensors right above the fog lights.

The lane-keeping system uses a camera that detects right and left lane markings. If the vehicle drives over a marking without the driver steering or using a turn signal, the system provides steering turns and warning alerts.

You can always see clearly behind the Denali with this high-res rear camera.

The Denali also has a high-**resolution** backup camera and GM's special-alert system. The system vibrates the driver's seat when the vehicle gets too close. The same alerts also indicate warnings from the lane-keeping alert system. The lane-keeping system instantly senses if the Denali wanders out of its highway lane.

ACTIVE SAFETY

The Denali's electronic marvels, of course, extend to active safety. Denali has front and rear automatic braking that uses short-range **radar**. The radar senses a collision and automatically stops the vehicle. "IntelliBeam" headlamps automatically adjust the high-beam lamps when oncoming traffic is detected. Denali owners can also purchase a special Teen Driver Mode that warns inexperienced drivers about any unsafe driving habits. Yukon's NavTraffic system displays traffic and road conditions and directs the driver toward the safest and most efficient route.

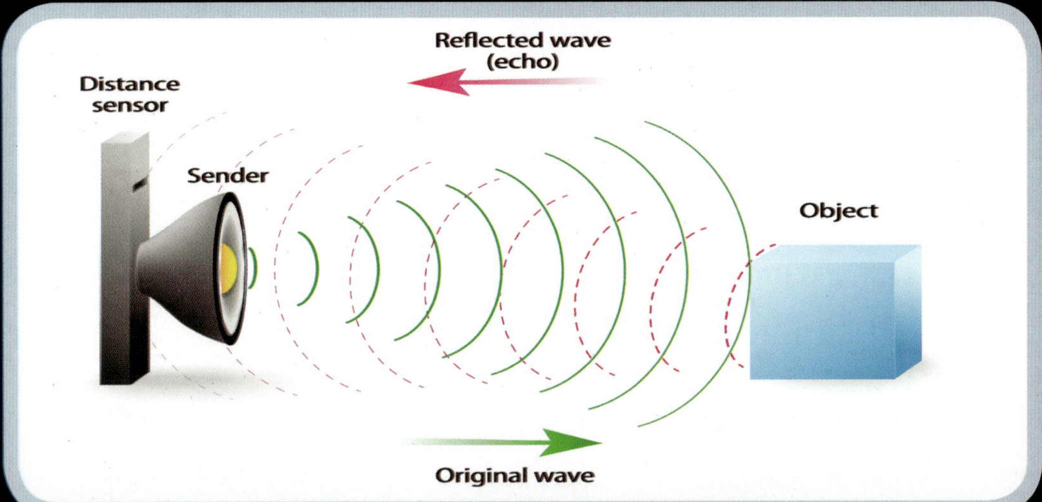

Radar is short for radio detection and ranging. Invented in the 1930s, radar sends out pulses of high-frequency waves that are reflected off an object, such as another car, and back to its source.

The first electric headlamps were introduced in 1898 on the Columbia Electric Car from the Electric Vehicle Company of Hartford, Connecticut, and were optional!

THE GM STORY

1993 GMC Yukon GT

General Motors Corporation was formed on September 16, 1908, in Flint, Michigan. At that time there were fewer than 8,000 automobiles in the United States. The company's first president was William C. Durant. In 1911, Durant started the Chevrolet motor company, which merged with GM in 1918. Other brands acquired by GM over the years include Cadillac, Buick, and Oldsmobile. By the early 1980s, GM employed more than 349,000 workers and operated 150 assembly plants around the world.

GMC introduced the Yukon in 1992. The Denali edition came along in 1999. General Motors today has four brands in the United States: Chevrolet, Buick, GMC, and Cadillac. In addition to the Yukon, GMC also builds all of GM's trucks.

1999 Yukon Denali

From 1931 through 2007, General Motors was the world's largest automaker. In 2008, Toyota surpassed GM in total sales.

THE NEAR FUTURE

Future Denali models will feature GM's Super Cruise. Now only available in GM's top-of-the-line Cadillacs, Super Cruise is the world's first truly hands-free driving system for highways. Once the driver turns on Super Cruise, it takes over, keeping the vehicle at a constant speed. It automatically slows down when approaching another car. It speeds up when passing.

One step beyond Super Cruise is a completely self-driving car. A self-driving car is one that is capable of sensing its environment and navigating without human input at all.

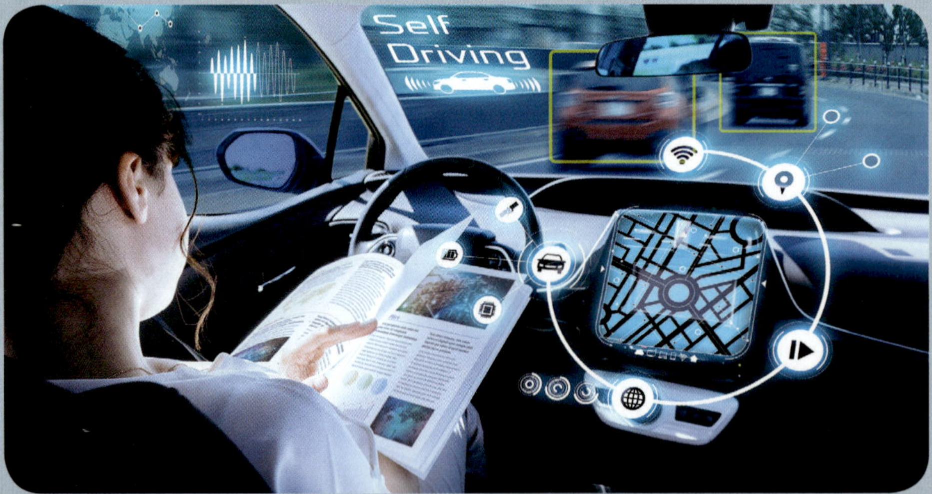

Even though the driver doesn't touch the steering wheel, he or she has to pay attention. Special software tracks the driver's head and automatically alerts him when his eyes aren't on the road. If the driver ignores the warning lights, a voice command will tell him or her to pay attention. Continued failure to take over steering will cause the vehicle to slow and brake to a stop. The system then turns on **hazard** warning and calls an emergency telephone line.

GM is developing a self-driving car called the Chevrolet Bolt. In the next couple of years, GM hopes to have a number of Bolts able to pick up passengers and deliver them to city destinations without a human driver.

GLOSSARY

cargo (KAHR-goh): freight carried by a ship, plane, truck, or other vehicle

hazard (HAZ-urd): something that is dangerous or likely to cause problems

horsepower (HORS-pou-ur): a unit for measuring the power of an engine

proximity (prahk-SIM-i-tee): nearness in space, time, or relationship

radar (RAY-dahr): a way ships, planes, and other vehicles find solid objects by reflecting radio waves off them and by receiving the reflected waves

resolution (rez-uh-LOO-shuhn): a measure of the quality of an image

stylish (STY-lish): displaying the latest style, fashionable

torque (tork): a twisting force that causes rotation

tri-zone (try-zohn): covering each of three areas, as in tri-zone heating or cooling

V-8 (Vee-ate): an eight-cylinder gasoline engine with the cylinders organized like the letter V

INDEX

SHOW WHAT YOU KNOW

1. How much weight can the Denali tow?
2. What is the main advantage of tri-zone climate control?
3. What are the four GM brands in the United States?
4. Who was the first president of General Motors?
5. In the year that General Motors was founded, about how many cars were in the United States?

FURTHER READING

Arnold, Nick, *How Cars Work: The Interactive Guide to Mechanisms That Make a Car Move*, Running Press, 2013.

Colson, Rob, *Top Marques: SUVs and Off Roaders:* Wayland Publishers, 2016.

Zink, Bradley, *It Starts with a Key: How Cars Work:* CreateSpace Independent Publishing Platform, 2016.

ABOUT THE AUTHOR

Charles Piddock is the former Editor-in-Chief of Weekly Reader Corporation. He has written many books for both young people and adults. He and his wife live by a lake in south-central Maine.

Meet The Author!
www.meetREMauthors.com

www.rourkeeducationalmedia.com

PHOTO CREDITS: All photos © Blue Door Education except cover © GM; Header art © Petrosg; speedometer art © didis both from Shutterstock.com; page 4-5 By Darren Brode–Shutterstock.com; elephant page 7 By gualtiero boffi–Shutterstock.com; page 14 illustration © Denys Po/Shutterstock.com, Page 8-9 and 15 © Abdullah AlBargan Flickr.com https://creativecommons.org/licenses/by-nd/2.0/ page 23 © By Andrey Suslov / Shutterstock.com; page 24 page 21 © Designua/Dreamstime, page 25 courtesy Beaulieu National Motor Museum; page 26 © Karrmann https://creativecommons.org/licenses/by-sa/3.0/deed.en ; page 28 © By chombosan / Shutterstock.com, page 29 © Grzegorz Czapski / Shutterstock.com

Edited by: Keli Sipperley

Cover design by: Rhea Magaro-Wallace Interior design by: Nicola Stratford www.nicolastratford.com

Library of Congress PCN Data

GMC Yukon Denali / Charles Piddock
(*VROOM!* Hot SUVs)
ISBN 978-1-64156-477-9 (hard cover)
ISBN 978-1-64156-603-2 (soft cover)
ISBN 978-1-64156-717-6 (e-Book)
Library of Congress Control Number: 2018930697

Rourke Educational Media
Printed in the United States of America, North Mankato, Minnesota